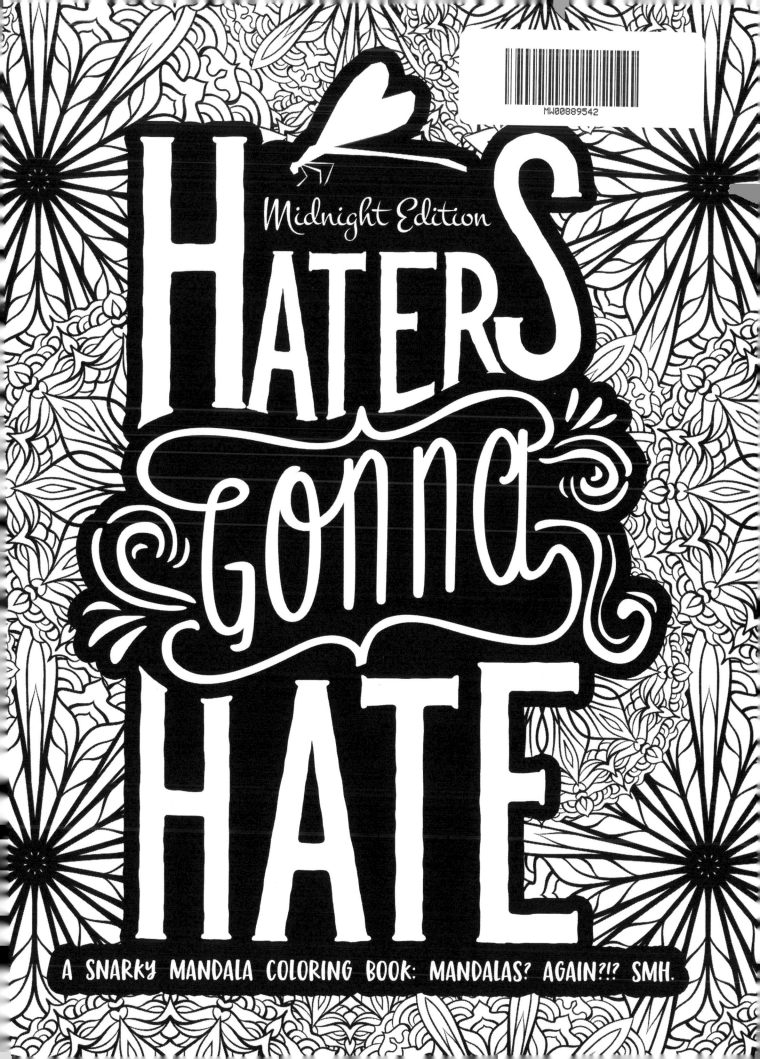

ISBN-13: 978-1533300379
ISBN-10: 1533300372

FREE DOWNLOAD

www.papeteriebleu.com/snarkymandala3

YOUR DOWNLOAD CODE: SN2397

@papeteriebleu

Papeterie Bleu

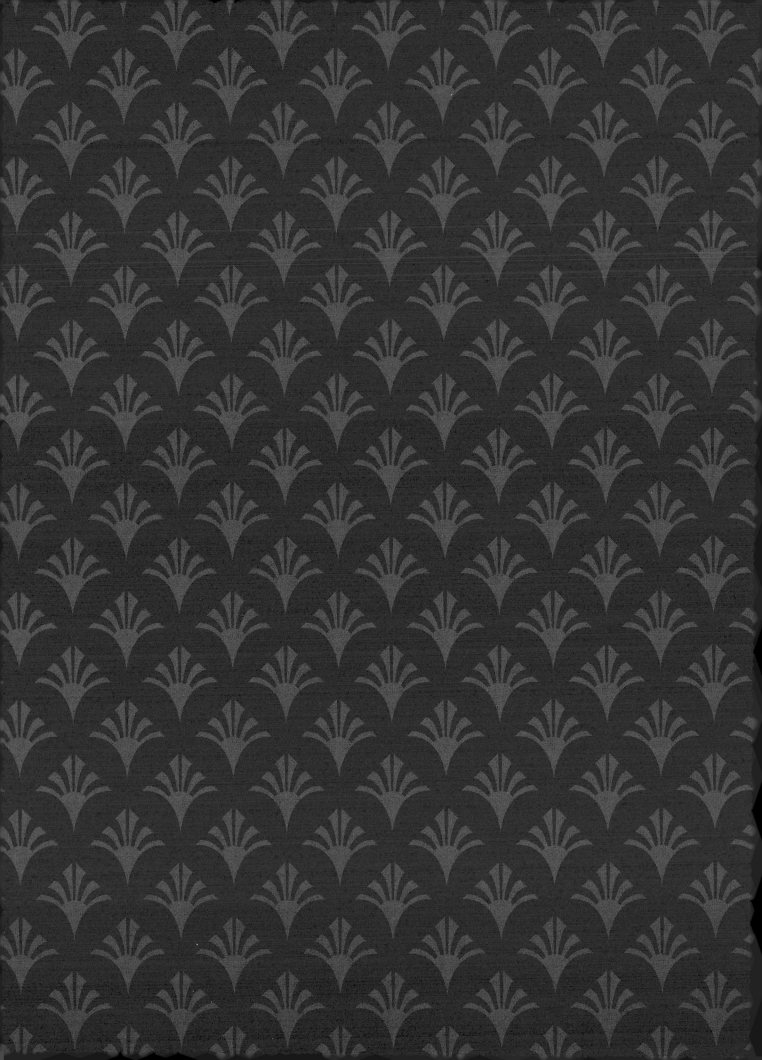

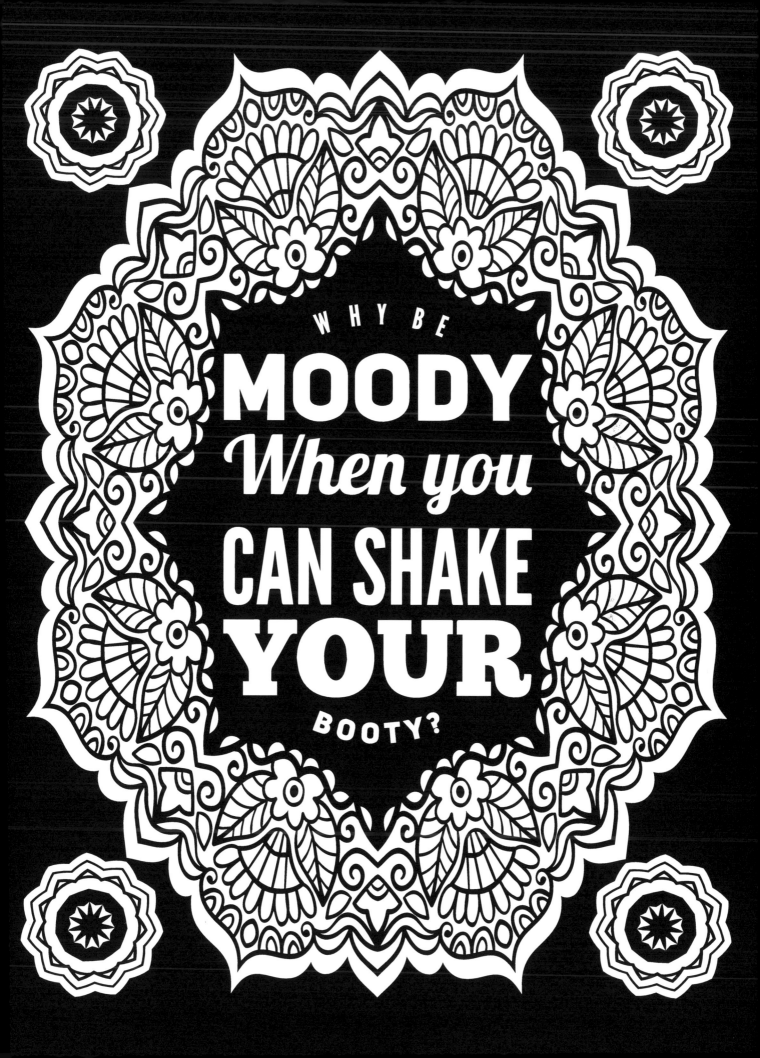

IF EVERY DAY *is a gift,* THEN TODAY WAS SOCKS

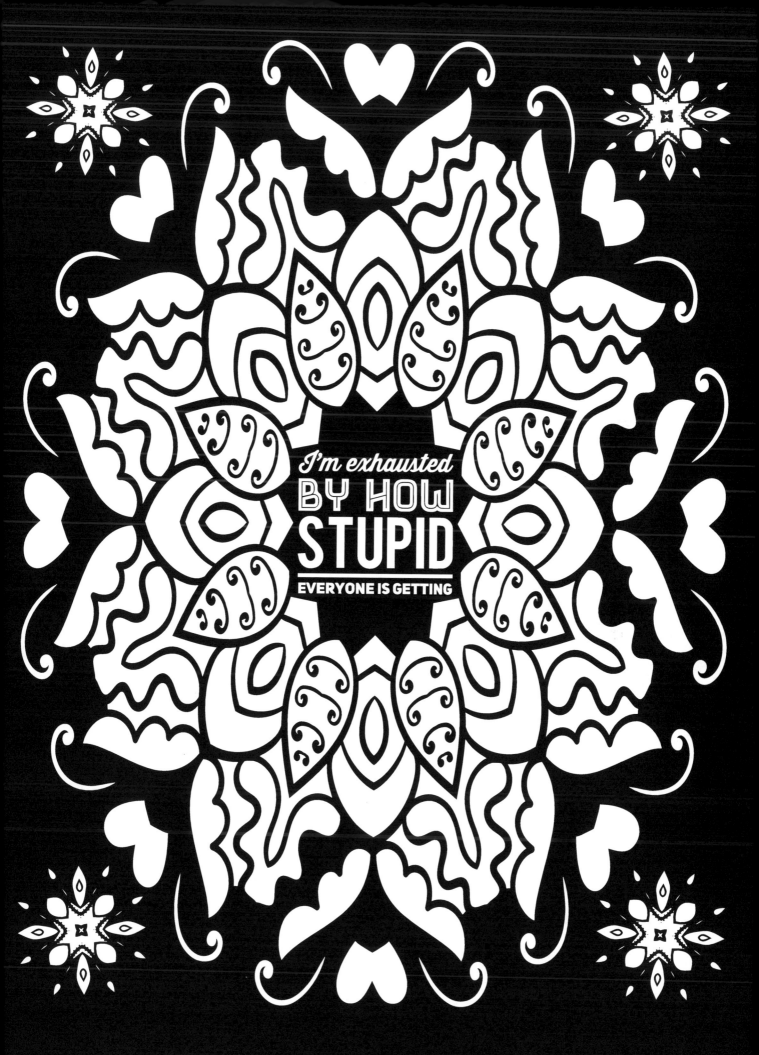

YOU'RE
AS USELESS
AS THE
"G"
IN LASAGNA

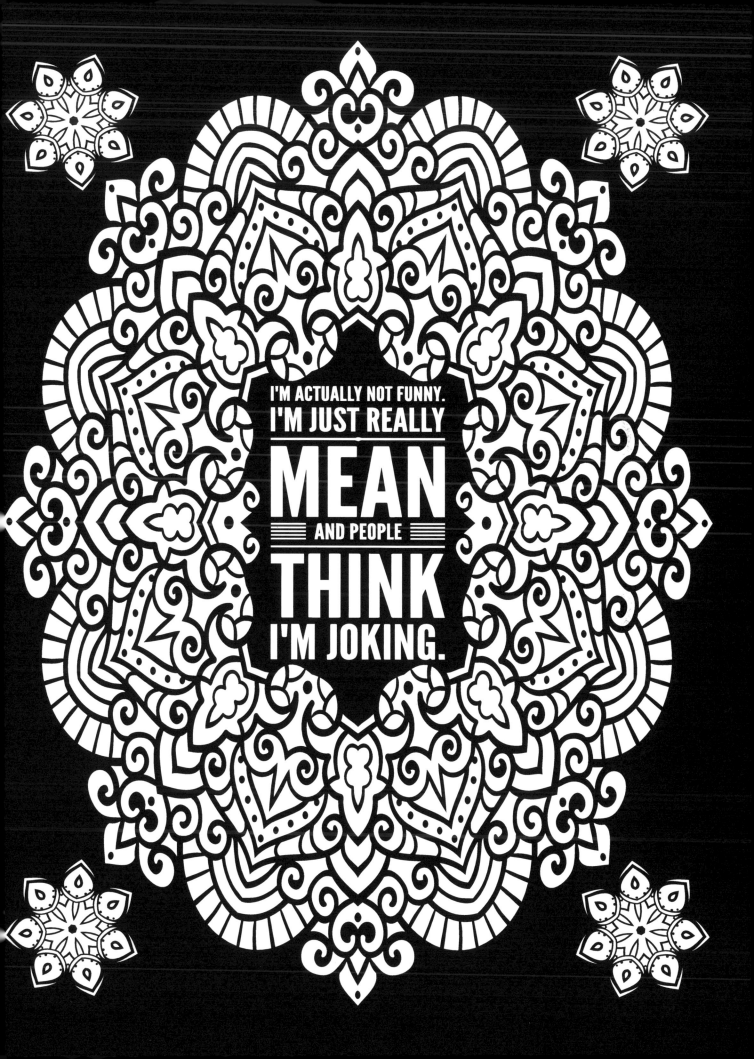

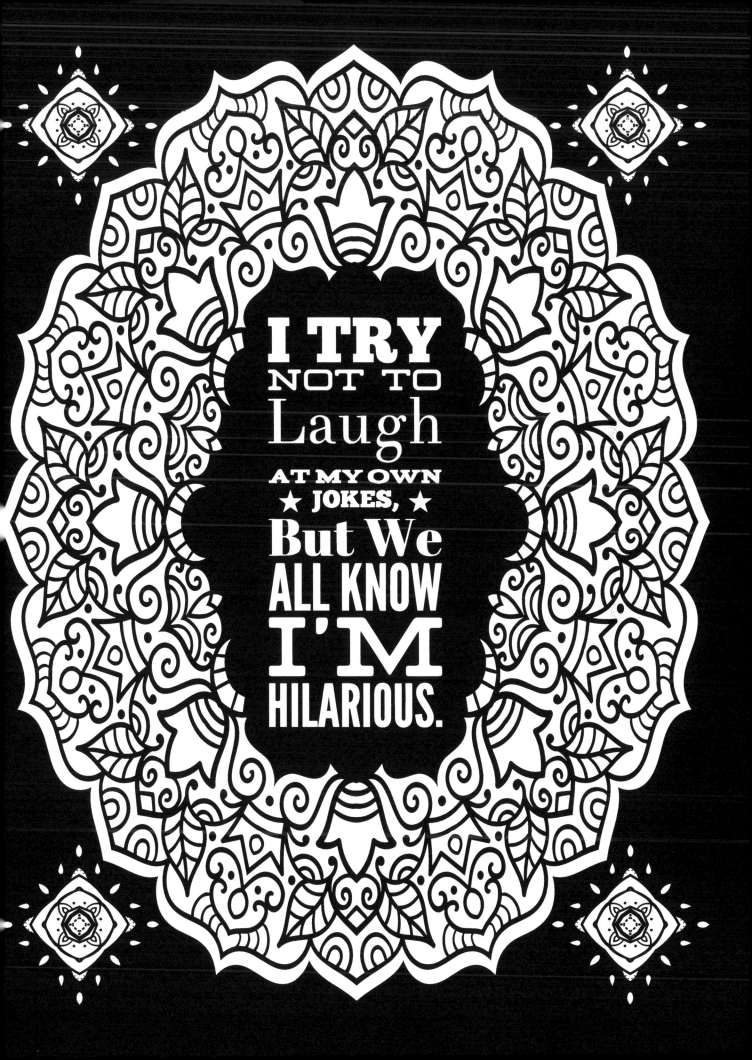

BE SURE TO FOLLOW US ON SOCIAL MEDIA FOR THE LATEST NEWS, SNEAK PEEKS, & GIVEAWAYS

@PapeterieBleu

Papeterie Bleu

@PapeterieBleu

ADD YOURSELF TO OUR MONTHLY NEWSLETTER FOR FREE DIGITAL DOWNLOADS AND DISCOUNT CODES

www.papeteriebleu.com/newsletter

CHECK OUT OUR OTHER BOOKS!

www.papeteriebleu.com

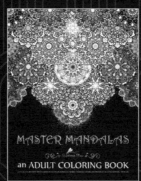

CHECK OUT OUR OTHER BOOKS!

www.papeteriebleu.com

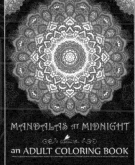

CHECK OUT OUR OTHER BOOKS!

www.papeteriebleu.com

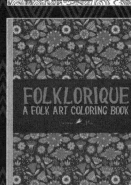

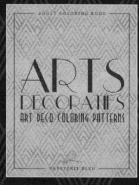

Made in the USA
Middletown, DE
23 November 2017